MICAH

MICAH
THE MIGHTY
MARATHONER

Mackenzie Snell

pictures by
Nathan Shields

BeaLu Books

To Stephen and Micah,
who continue to inspire me every day

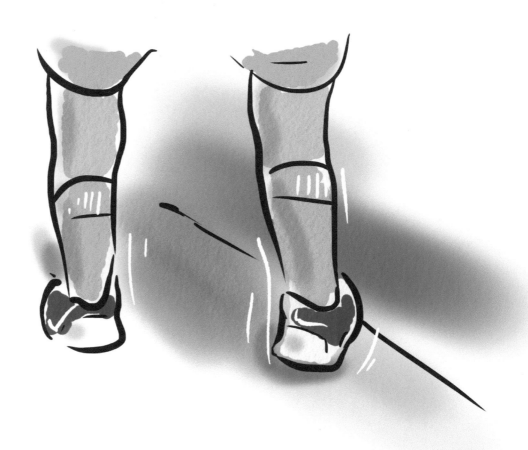

Micah loves to run.

But Micah does not run like most people.

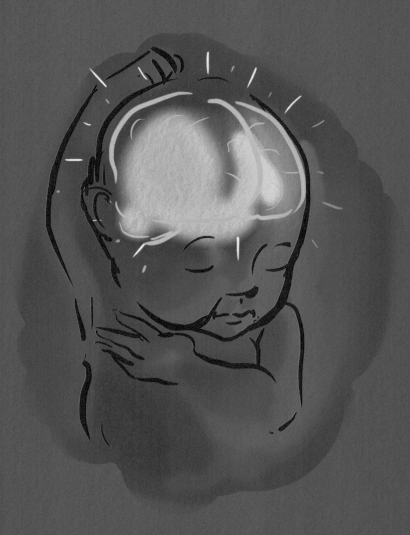

When Micah was born, his brain was made a little different. Micah stayed in the hospital for a very long time. It was very hard for Micah's family to see him in the hospital every day. They were all so happy when he got to go home.

Our brains have two different sides that talk to each other to help us be able to move, speak, and play.

One side of Micah's brain doesn't talk very well to the other side of his brain. It makes moving, speaking, and playing hard.

Even though Micah's brain is a little different, he still likes many of the same things any other kid would. He loves to play and loves his friends and family.

Micah really enjoys music. He loves to go to concerts and music class at school. Sometimes he plays music with his sister.

Going to school is something else Micah also really loves. Some of Micah's favorite parts of school are going to recess, doing art, talking with his friends, and reading stories.

Micah is still learning how to stand and walk and run. He gets lots of help from his physical therapists and special equipment, but Micah still works hard.

Even though Micah does not run on his feet, he gets to run with his dad when he pushes him in a super cool wheelchair called Orange Crush. It is bright orange and made to go very fast when it is pushed.

Micah rolls in really long races called marathons. These races can take more than four hours and are 26.2 miles long! They do marathons in all sorts of cool places!

During these long races, Micah has his running buddies Monkey and Tiger to keep him company. Tiger and Monkey are always looking out for him.

When Micah gets tired during his races, Monkey and Tiger cheer, "Go Micah!" and "You can do it!" They love to meet other racers while they roll.

Sometimes, the weather isn't great when Micah is racing. It rains. And it is cold. But that doesn't stop Mighty Micah! Orange Crush has a special clear cover that keeps Micah dry, and his racing buddies and orange blanket help him stay warm.

Micah has lots of fans who come to watch him and his dad race. They all wear orange shirts because orange is Micah's favorite color.

At the end of a race, Micah gets a shiny gold medal.

All of Micah's family and friends give him great big hugs, especially his mom!

After a big race, Micah is always tired and likes to take a nap with his racing buddies.

Micah, Monkey, and Tiger don't race just because Micah likes to run. They make up Team Micah's Miles, and together they race in marathons to raise awareness and money for charities. They love racing together and helping others.

Learn More About Micah and Micah's Miles

The Snell family's journey with Micah didn't go according to plan. He made his entrance into this world seven and a half weeks early and stayed in the NICU for thirty-eight days. Life began to blur with doctors, specialists, medicines, and diagnosis. Micah's mom, Suzie, became the expert on sharing Micah's medical history in three to five minutes, over and over and over again. They learned about seizures and seizure medications. They learned about feeding tubes. Really, they just learned to survive.

The world constantly told them what Micah couldn't do, and it seemed like the only thing the Snells could do was just listen. Without the support of family and friends, they are not sure where they'd be. After a while, life started to settle into a new routine. They met other families who had similar experiences; they met organizations like the United Cerebral Palsy Foundation. Most importantly, they didn't feel as alone. The Snells were ready to start pushing back on the constant message of what Micah couldn't do because Micah is an amazing kid that can do so much.

Micah had always loved to be outside riding in a stroller, and the Snells really liked taking him on walks and for runs. Micah's dad, Jeff, was training for a marathon, and they thought; why not take Micah? As they planned for the marathon, they started thinking about how they could use the experience they had to raise awareness and funds for some of the organizations that supported Micah. With that first marathon, Micah's Miles was born with the mission of building a community around Micah and inspiring others through his amazing spirit.

For each marathon, Micah partners with a cause that makes a difference for others. At eight years old, Micah has finished twenty-six marathons and raised over $60,000 for the partner organizations. Micah has the spirit of a runner; he understands perseverance and patience. It's really all he knows. That runner's spirit is a little light that shines out from him.

The Snells have the amazing opportunity to share Micah with the world. Micah's Miles brings people together and reminds them constantly of what a gift life is. They are very fortunate to have a Micah's Miles Team which consists of friends, family, and community leaders who have come together to help us share Micah's story. Micah's sister, Mackenzie, and brother, Stephen are a big part of Micah's life as well as grandparents and extended family. Micah loves school, and all his teachers and friends. He loves watching the Seattle Seahawks and Gonzaga Bulldogs and all his siblings' activities. He's also a huge fan of music and musicals.

This book is a glimpse into Micah through the eyes of his sister. The Snell's hope it brings you joy and inspires you to share your light with others.

Micah, Mackenzie, and Suzie use this book in assemblies they present at schools. Micah uses a communication device to help with the lesson. They teach about the character trait perseverance by reading the story and sharing three themes from Micah's life: don't give up, working hard can be fun, and make a team. We hope you and your students enjoy reading Micah the Mighty Marathoner and lesson on perseverance, hard work, and teamwork.

Micah the Mighty Marathoner
Perseverance, Hard Work, Teamwork

Learning Targets:
Students will be able to understand what perseverance is through examples from Micah's story.
Students will be able to understand and give examples of how hard work can be fun.
Students will be able to state who they would choose to be on their team in a challenging situation.

Before Reading:
Show students the cover of Micah the Mighty Marathoner and ask:
- What inferences can you make?
- What predictions can you make about the book?
- What do you know about marathons?
- Who is Micah?

During Reading:
Show students the pictures as you read. Stop and answer any questions the children may have as you are reading.

After Reading:
Use the questions to guide your students in a classroom conversation or circle discussion about Micah the Mighty Marathoner and perseverance:
- What was one thing you took away or learned from this book?
- What was your favorite part of this book and why?
- What is perseverance?
- How does Micah show perseverance?
- Does Micah have to work hard to learn new things?
- Do you have to work hard at learning new things?
- Give students an example such as learning to ride their bike or something similar.

- Was it hard at first?
- Did you crash once? Twice? More?
- Allow students to tell stories
- When you were finally successful, was it worth ALL that work?
- Stress that hard work can be fun—during and especially after you have learned your new skill.
- Have you ever been in a challenging situation?
- Allow students to tell stories about their challenging situations.
- Then listen for who they talk about in their stories (parents, teachers, friends, etc.).
- Does Micah have a team to help him when things become challenging?
- Who is on his team?
- Who is on your team?
- Go back to one of the students who told a story about their challenging situation and review the people that helped them. Tell the student that these people are on their team.
- Then ask, why are they on your team?
- Why is it important to have a team?

Closing:
- Restate the meaning of perseverance, hard work, and the importance of a team.
- Highlight some examples students shared during the lesson and make connections to Micah's story.
- Challenge students to think about a future situation where perseverance, hard work, and a team may be important. Ask how they could approach the situation using what they learned today.

About the Author

Mackenzie Snell is currently a student at Camas High School in Camas, Washington. She loves to play soccer, which she does both competitively and with the Special Olympics at school. Mackenzie loves to help children with disabilities which is one reason she thinks that she is so fortunate to have a brother like Micah. Mackenzie wants to be a doctor someday so she can continue to help people. Mackenzie also has a twin brother, Stephen, and a chocolate lab named Clara, she loves spending time with them both, sometimes more with Clara than Stephen. :-)

About the Illustrator

Nathan Shields likes making art with his family in Port Angeles, Washington.

Proceeds from the sale of this book will go to Micah's Miles partner charities. Visit MicahsMiles.org for more information.

Copyright © 2018

ISBN: 978-0-9990924-3-9

Library of Congress Control Number: 2018953230

Edited by: Luana K. Mitten
Book cover and design by Tara Raymo • creativelytara.com

Printed in the United States of America
September 2018

BeaLu Books
Tampa, Florida

www.BeaLuBooks.com

CPSIA information can be obtained
at www.ICGtesting.com
Printed in the USA
LVHW07n1926231018
594592LV00001B/3/P